Remembering Grandma Moses

"Grandma Moses," a portrait by Lisel Salzer, 1947.

Remembering Grandma Moses

by Beth Moses Hickok

Images from the Past
Bennington, Vermont

Artist Lisel Salzer, now a resident of Seattle, Washington, and herself 87 years old in 1994, recalled the circumstances under which she painted the portrait of Grandma Moses that appears on the frontispiece:

The portrait was painted, if I remember rightly, in August 1947, in the beginning of her fame.

My husband and I were driving back to New York after a vacation in Maine. On the way we visited friends in Eagle Bridge. They told us about Grandma Moses and asked, "Would you like to visit her?" Of course we did.

We arrived at her house early afternoon and she received us in a white lace dress. She was "love at first sight," charming and inspiring.

I had one canvas left in our car, and I immediately asked her whether she would allow me to paint her.

She said that she could not afford it. (I think she had 36 grandchildren or so at that time.)

I told her I would not want her to pay for it, I just would love to paint her. Then she said her art dealer might not allow it. It so happened that I knew her art dealer — and she finally agreed. I asked Grandma Moses, would she like to paint while I painted her? She replied that she'd rather "pose like a lady"!

And she did. She sat silently in an old armchair, not moving at first. Then she relaxed and started talking, and her talk had exactly the same charm as her painting — about her past, but also about her new career.

She said she had to live at least six more years, to outlive the contract with her art dealer — he got too much money! (Of course, she did, but then my guess is she renewed the contract.)

After all, she started out selling her paintings in the local drug store, together with her raspberry jam, for a dollar apiece.

The painting was finished in one day and at the end, she told me that I was the first real artist she had met!

It was a great adventure for me and it seemed she had fun, too.

[Ms. Salzer has bequeathed the portrait to the Bennington Museum.]

ISBN 1-884592-01-5

Book design by Christopher Kuntze
Text of "Remembering Grandma Moses" copyright © 1994 by Beth Moses Hickok
Entire publication copyright © 1994 by Beech Seal Press

LIBRARY OF CONGRESS CATALOGUING-IN-PUBLICATION DATA

Hickok, Beth Moses,
    Remembering Grandma Moses / by Beth Moses Hickok.
        p.   cm.
    ISBN 1-884592-01-5 : $12.95
    1. Moses, Grandma, 1860–1961. 2. Painters–United States–
Biography.   I. Title.
ND237.M78H53   1994
759.13–dc20   94-24919
    [B]   CIP

IMAGES FROM THE PAST
Tordis Ilg Isselhardt Publisher
Printed in the United States of America
9998   432

Contents

Grandma Moses, photographed in 1949 by Christina Stevens.

HOOSICK TOWNSHIP HISTORICAL SOCIETY

Introduction

This reminiscence brings intimate new perspective to bear on a legendary American personality. The author deftly commingles diverse time elements so that one can read in the 1990s a manuscript written in the 1960s that brings back to life episodes and dialogue that took place in the 1930s about an Upper New York State farmwife who was about to become famous.

At one level it is a simple story, that of a young woman deciding whether to marry a widower, twelve years older than she, who has two young daughters and whose mother-in-law proves to be a powerful presence. At another level we are transported into the home, in Bennington, Vermont, during the Great Depression, of Grandma Moses only a few years before she is "discovered" as a master primitive artist who gains international renown. At still a third level, this is a sociological narrative about a peppery, no-nonsense New Englander, born before the Civil War, who has lost half of the ten infants to whom she has given birth, and about the many earthy skills with which she cooks, cleans, sews, paints, economizes, runs the household, and handles human relations.

Such a fertile mixture of layered interpretation is usually the stuff of fiction; yet here we have pure fact, gently recalled by a member of the family as skilled with words as the subject was with paint.

As a matter of fact, both author and subject share certain other characteristics, though they were unrelated and separated by more than a half century of age. Small in stature, energetic in nature, canny in the ways of the world, and opinionated on certain subjects, both left home relatively young to earn a livelihood. Both also share talents in different fields that deserve recognition and accolade.

Grandma Moses gained renown as a public figure starting in the late 1930s and she lived in good health and spirits to see her 100th birthday in 1960 become a veritable national holiday. By the time of her death, more than a year later, she had inspired generations of senior citizens to follow their fancies, indulge their talents, and be true to their own personalities and interests. It was a remarkable American life, and remains a story worthy of reflection.

The author's story is centered on 1934 when she was making the decision whether to marry Frank Moses, who was — as she explains in some detail — both Grandma's nephew and son-in-law. Reading between the lines, we think that her decision already had pretty well been made.

The fact that Beth and Frank did marry, and then Beth became stepmother to Grandma Moses's two young granddaughters, Zoan and Frances, allowed Grandma to leave residential Bennington, where she had been the interim stepmother, and return to the farm she much preferred, just over the state line in Eagle Bridge, New York.

When this recollection was written in the 1960s, Frank and Beth Moses had sold their Bulrushes Motor Court, off Route 9 just west of Bennington, and were preparing to retire. Frank was quite ill and Beth wished to be involved in activities that would let her stay near him. She enrolled in the Famous Writers School of Westport, Connecticut, which was then advertising widely in magazines and other media, even on matchbook covers, likely to attract would-be scribes. Beth thrived on the correspondence course, read all the material and texts that were included, and enjoyed the experience greatly. Every eight weeks a different tutor-writer would be assigned, and in an attempt to personalize the relationship, each student was given a photograph of the temporary teacher.

For her final paper, a major work that was to be 5,500 words in length, the instructor at the time, noting the family connection, suggested that she write on the subject of Grandma Moses. "Easy," Beth remembers thinking. "Fifty-five hundred words? I could have written fifty-five thousand words about Grandma — all the stories I'd heard, all the things she said."

Grandma, it seemed, loved to tell stories, especially funny ones, and had a special gift for embellishment. At the time this recollection was written, in the early 1960s, Grandma had recently died at the age of 101, and therefore Beth thought that it would serve several good purposes to put it all on paper.

The instructor liked the article and suggested that she try to sell it for publication. A practical problem was that 5,500 words is too long for a magazine article, too short for the usual book. The manuscript languished.

As to how direct quotes and dialogue could be reconstructed after the passage of so much time, the author's explanation is triply credible. One reason is that some of the quotes came from correspondence with Beth's mother which had been kept over the years. "My mother would keep our letters; each was kind of a story of our life. We all wrote to her often, at least once a week." A second reason she remembered the dialogue was that, "I was young, and I was interested in her. If Grandma talked to you, you wouldn't forget it . . . Sometimes they were about things that were very touchy. I would never forget her sitting and telling me about having that baby that died . . . You know, you just don't forget things like that. Grandma, actually, was a wonderful story teller. Told me and Frank scads of stories about the family and growing up down on the farm." A third reason is that Beth kept her detailed diaries and was able simply to quote from them years later.

One of the stories Beth recalls demonstrated how "Grandma was always one jump ahead of her children." Thomas, Grandma's husband, who died in 1927, was different — a very gentle, kindly, and loving man who had eyes over which the youngsters could, to recirculate an old cliche, pull some wool. "But they never fooled Grandma," Beth said.

The yarn she relates was that in the days before refrigeration, Grandma had a regular pantry as well as a cold pantry, or coolroom, where the ice box was located. (Note that this means not a refrigerator but a box that was cooled by keeping a block of ice in it.) One time, as was her custom, she made up about ten pies at once — apple, blueberry, and cherry — and stored them for a while in the coolroom. This time the boys, probably her sons Hughie, Forrest, and Loyd, swiped one of the pies from the coolroom, devoured it, then cleaned and returned the plate thinking that Grandma would never notice or count the pies.

Beth continues the tale: "The next week she waited, and when she heard them in the coolroom, she locked the door on them. They were in there for a good, long time, and couldn't get out. She finally let them out and made it known that she didn't appreciate such thievery. The girls were mixed up in it too, although they didn't get locked in the coolroom."

Another story about Grandma's "in charge" attitude toward her household comes from Mary Hard Bort, a resident of Manchester, Vermont, who grew up across Bennington's Elm Street from the Moses family. One of Mary's recollections was of making a "Sunday call," with her parents, on Grandma Moses after she had moved back to Eagle Bridge. "I remember vividly two things about that visit: Grandma Moses wore around her waist a belt to which was attached a large ring of keys that rested in her apron pocket (I wanted desperately to know what those keys unlocked but dared not ask). And I remember her parlor where we sat and where she directed me to sit in a specific chair and look at some stereoptican views. I finished quickly (they weren't very interesting) and was ready for something else but Grandma told me curtly to sit where I was, look at them again and be quiet. I seem to remember it as a fairly brief visit. I still wonder what those keys were for."

Grandma was not about to be manipulated by any

children, whether members of her own family or others. She locked the pie thieves in the coolroom for a good long time to teach them a lesson. She forced Mary Bort to look at boring stereo views, then told her to do it again, and do it quietly. She certainly earned that reputation for pepperiness.

"How could I have known," Mary now asks, "that the lady who came to take care of my friends Zoan and Frances would one day be the most famous grandmother in the country?"

Mary Bort continues, "My father and Frank Moses were friends, as were my mother and Ann (also known as Anna). I loved to spend time at 218 Elm Street partly because the girls had a sandbox at the side of the house and we were often playing there when Frank called home at the end of the day. He usually stopped to talk to us, and he called me Mazzooweeze, rather than Mary Louise as other adults did. I adored him. Besides the sandbox, the girls had a big basement with a swing suspended from the ceiling and plenty of clean dry space to play. How I envied them. (Beth says it was she who installed the big swing to hang from the floor joists in the cellar.)

"When their Grandma came, she came to care for their dying mother, but the three of us did not know that. I just remember a tiny lady who paid little attention to us, and though she was not unkind, she had a crisp, no-nonsense way of speaking. I saw her most often working in the kitchen or doing needlework of some kind."

Mary Bort also remembers the small yarn picture of a house which Grandma had made (featured on the cover of this book) which Grandma gave to Beth as a wedding present. The yarn painting hung on a narrow wall near the dining room doorway. "I was impressed that she had 'made up a picture,' for no one in my family did that," Mary remembers.

"Some time after Grandma came," she continues, "everything changed. Ann died (my mother cried, which was a rare occurrence), my sister was born (I hadn't expected that), and we moved back to Manchester (the Depression had affected my father's business and he was needed at the farm)."

What did Beth know about Grandma's paintings before their "discovery"? Only that she had done some casual painting, using any old paint available as well as any old piece of plywood or leftover board, even a piece of sheet metal. She would stash these items on shelves under the stairs to the cellar of the house in Bennington. Some of the paintings she left were swept up with the trash and sent off to the town dump. Recalls Beth now: "Who was to know? Nobody knew that she was going to be 'discovered.' Otto Kallir (the New York gallery owner) told me afterwards that we had placed at least $125,000 worth of Grandma Moses paintings in the dump."

After Grandma's art was discovered, Beth remembers, "Grandma became famous so fast, she really didn't have time for any of us, even the children. It became a family saying, how Grandma would tell everyone, 'I'm famous now, you know.'"

To help the reader make factual connections in this selective tale, there is included a chronology of relevant dates and events.

Remembering Grandma Moses

The worn, red, leather-bound diary lies before me on Great-grandfather Moses's old red cherry desk. I do not need it, except to quote accurately, for I remember her as though it were yesterday.

Grandma Moses was sitting in a circle of light from a bridge lamp that was close to her small black, ladder-backed chair. The rest of the floor was in darkness. Grandma was saving electricity. A portable Singer sewing machine sat on a sturdy low, oak stand in front of her. It was held firmly in place with a clamp, because Grandma sewed with the vigor she put into all tasks. Across her lap and flowing over the stand to the floor was a gaily colored patchwork quilt. Its size accentuated her tiny bent figure.

I thought Grandma was very old. She did look more than her 74 years, and I was only 23. This was on December 26, 1934.

Her hair was entirely gray, long and thin, piled in a flat pug on the very top of her head. Her forehead was high, above her round, gold-framed glasses that covered the most expressive, bright, hazel eyes I had ever seen. The flesh over her cheekbones was firm and round and rose colored. Her nose, slightly Roman, was a well-shaped one. Deep lines ran to the base of her round chin and there were two soft packets of flesh that sagged below each side. Her face was patterned with work lines.

She wore a flowered print housedress with a hem about six inches from the floor, along with black, soft, low-heeled Montgomery Ward oxfords and black cotton stockings. Her shoulders and arms were snugly covered by an old-fashioned, purple wool hug-me-tight. The house was very warm, but she explained that all her life she had gone from her warm, quilted, feather-ticked bed to a freezing-cold farm kitchen, and the memories of the drafts and ice-cold iron range remained so vivid that she shivered without the customary cozy garment.

"What on earth are you doing up, all dressed and sewing at four o'clock in the morning?" I asked.

She looked up at me with her head on one side, like a sassy sparrow, and answered, "And what are you doing down here in your night clothes?"

"I heard the machine. It sounded like whirr-bump, whirr-bump. It makes a thump when it stops suddenly. I see now that it is because of the short seams of the quilt pieces. It's pitch dark out, Grandma.''

"I went to bed at a Christian hour, wasn't out ramming around all night," she snapped.

I drew my robe tightly around me and remembered my mother's warnings about not answering Grandma back.

Frank, her nephew and son-in-law, and I had come in before midnight after coffee with friends he wanted me to meet.

"The first thing I ever sewed was a quilt for my doll's cradle," I said. "My Grandma Stuart cut out the squares and I had to sew them together with an over-and-over stitch."

"Oh! You sew?" she asked.

"Yes, and I like it very much. If I wanted clothes I had to. I'm a country farm girl too, you know."

Thus began the second day of my Christmas vacation visit. I drew up a dining chair and sat down beside her.

"I s'pose you're set on marrying Frank." Grandma leaned back and held two quilt pieces in tensed hands — small, thin, blue-veined, arthritic, creative, workworn hands.

"That's what I'm here to decide. I love him and he is very lonely. He loved your Anna, so it is worse for him than it would be for a man who had not got on with his wife. It is almost three years but because of the age difference (Frank was 34) and the fact that I have not finished the education my family expects of me, plus the responsibility of little girls, seven and eight and a half, it is not something to take lightly. Because of my big family and the Depression, I feel old for my age."

"So?" She seemed to be waiting.

"First I must get acquainted with Zoan and Frances and see if they want me."

" 'Course they want ya now. It's all kisses and buttermilk, but what-cha going to do comes time they need a lickin'?"

I laughed. "Lickin's will have to be in Frank's department. Gosh, Grandma, I only weigh 105 pounds. I might get the worst of that deal."

She chuckled and I wondered if perhaps she envisioned that possibility with a bit of relish.

"Frank says you're anxious to go home to your farm in Eagle Bridge."

"I certainly do want to go home," she declared. "I've been away too long now. I have things I want to do.

Maybe I'm homesick, don't like village livin' and never did."

"I understand how you feel about the girls. They'll miss you and naturally you'll worry about them but you can have them visit and you'll always be welcome here."

" 'Course I'll worry but I've brought up so many young'uns I'm tired of it. Once'st I know they're in good hands, I'll be satisfied. Hugh's three kids are at the farm but they're Dorothy's job, not mine. I don't plan to do much visitin'. . . .' " She shook out the quilt with a snap. "As I say, I have things I mean to do."

(Little did either of us dream of all she was to do in the next twenty-seven years!)

For the next thirty-six years I've been trying to explain my relationship to Grandma Moses but it still confuses everyone, so I'll start at the beginning.

Her full name was Anna Mary Robertson Moses, but almost everyone called her Grandma.

There were three Moses brothers: William, Thomas, and Walter. Thomas was Grandma's husband. Walter was my husband Frank's father. William and Walter settled in Vermont. Thomas and his bride, Anna Mary, went to a farm in Staunton, Virginia, where they had ten

The author in 1935, age 23, with her new stepdaughters, Zoan, 10, and Frances, 8, and the gambrel-roofed home on Elm Street in Bennington, Vermont, where they lived. It was here in 1927 that Grandma Moses began to care for her ailing daughter, Anna, who died of tuberculosis in 1933. The house looks much the same today, but the octagonal stepping stones built by Frank Moses no longer make up the front walk.

Two snapshots from a family album of Frances and Zoan Moses about 1935 at the time their widowed father was remarried; and a studio portrait taken by a commercial photographer, Wills T. White.

children. Five lived, and five were either stillborn or died in infancy. Thomas and Mary suffered a heavy loss when their Staunton house burned, and they were home-sick for Eagle Bridge, New York.

Walter and William prospered. In 1905 Walter found and bought the Eagle Bridge farm for Thomas, and sent for him. It was a good farm. Thomas and Anna Mary came with their children: Ona, Loyd, Forrest, Anna, and Hughie. They worked from sunup to sundown and paid for the farm in a very few years.

Walter and his sons, Paul and Frank, helped out, spending a great deal of time there. As time went on, Frank and Anna fell deeply in love. There was an awful row because they were cousins, so they eloped to The Little Church Around the Corner. Grandma never seemed to mind as much as the others.

Grandpa Walter, who was a carpenter by trade, gave them a house lot next to his home on Elm Street in Bennington, Vermont, and helped them to build a beautiful home.

Anna had been in nurse's training but was forced to give up because of a bout with tuberculosis. Her case had been arrested but their two little girls came close, one after the other. Frank and his Dad worked against time to get her into the new home. In 1933 Anna died. Grandma Anna Mary, who was by then a widow, stayed on after Anna's long sickness, kept house, and took care of Zoan and Frances.

Grandma was Frank's aunt by marriage, his mother-in-law via Anna, and she was Zoan and Frances's maternal grandmother, for they are double Moseses.

I met Frank early in 1934. I visited, or rather called at, his home briefly on two occasions. We took the little girls on outings during the summer. By fall, Frank had asked me to marry him. Each of his daughters had made a week's visit to my family home in Massachusetts. Frank's father approved heartily. But Grandma knew others she would rather have for a stepmother to the girls.

I said, "I will go to Bennington and spend Christmas vacation with you all and see if marriage will be right for all of us." That's how the ten days came about.

Christmas Day 1934

The mountains were deep purple, the sky blue-gray, and it was snowing gently as we drove through the Berkshires. The scenes were pure romance, the essence of the New England dream Christmas.

These rag dolls, made by Grandma Moses and given to her granddaughters Frances and Zoan for Christmas 1934, were later donated to the Bennington Museum as part of its extensive collection of Grandma Moses paintings and memorabilia. BENNINGTON MUSEUM

*Frank (1898—1971) in a photo taken in his 60s, Anna Moses
Moses (1899—1933), and their gravestone in Park Lawn
Cemetery, Bennington, Vermont.*

The little girls greeted me with excited hugs, Grandma with old-fashioned hospitality. Most of the rooms in the white house, with its four sturdy green gables, were still stark-white, unpapered hard plaster. The oak floors were waxed and buffed to a mirror surface. There was a tall, brightly lighted but sparsely trimmed Christmas tree in the corner of the large living room.

Grandma led me up the winding staircase to the spotless master bedroom that reached across the entire front of the house. She showed me the modern bath, children's room, sunporch, and her small bedroom, next to mine.

"This is a lovely house," I said. "How nicely you keep it, Grandma."

"It's got all the modern conveniences," she answered. "Walter and Frank don't spare the horses none when they're building, and I ain't too old to keep house, not yit."

"I just love the bay window and the window seat. I've always liked light and sunshine in a house."

She bustled about, opening a drawer for me to use, and opening both of the walk-in closets at each end of the room.

"Anna's coats and a few of her dresses and such are still hanging here." She looked straight at me as though measuring my reaction.

Not knowing what to say, I just kept quiet.

"They's some Frank's age who like bay winders too," she snapped.

"Grandma, I . . . I can well understand how you feel. I came here to decide what to do and I hope you will help me. Can't we be friends?"

At this she smiled, and her sharp hazel eyes twinkled. "Well, we kin try." With that she whirled and trotted off down the stairs, calling over her shoulder, "You best wash up in a hurry. I'm a-goin' to put dinner on right off."

A few great, lazy snowflakes drifted down, but afternoon sun shone through the triple-mullion windows on the west wall of the dining room and onto the Christmas table, set with white, Roman gold-rimmed, hand-painted china and delicate old linen.

Zoan said, "Our mother painted these dishes and fired them in her own kiln at the farm."

"They're beautiful, dear," I said. "We must be very careful of them so that you and Frances can have them when you grow up. Such a big and complete set, you can both have plenty. She must have been a fine artist."

Oh, what a dinner that was. We began with tall,

sparkling goblets of freshly squeezed orange juice, followed by roast capon, stuffed with old-fashioned bread dressing, light, dry, and oniony. There were fluffy mashed potatoes, buttered steamed squash, golden boiled onions, turnip, candied sweet potatoes, carrot and cabbage salad, freshly baked yeast rolls, cranberry sauce, three kinds of pickles, celery, olives, nuts, mince pie, pumpkin pie, sage cheese, sharp rat-trap cheese, chocolate and divinity fudge, half English walnuts filled with fondant, stuffed dates, peanut brittle from an old Virginia recipe, and a ten-cup, agate-wear pot of fragrant boiled coffee.

"Grandma! I'm breathless! I have never had a more bountiful or delicious dinner in my life. You're the world's best cook."

"The Moseses," she declared, "are always good providers. Their womanfolk are expected to set a good table."

Was this meant as instruction? I wondered.

Frank spoke up. "Aunt Mary does a heap of canning, jelly making and pickling, and nobody on this earth can make raised rolls to beat hers. Not even to match them."

"If I laid-um end-ta-end, that I've raised, they'd reach from here to Californee," she chuckled.

"Do you mind the time, Frank, I put the big padlock on the cold-pantry door, to keep you boys out and you swiped ya father's hacksaw and sawed it off?" Turning to me with laughing eyes, "Those duffers et six pies I'd set up for weekend comp'nee."

Frank remembered, the children giggled, and I encouraged their reminiscences to learn what I could of their family background.

I suddenly remembered Grandpa Walter Moses and his sister next door. "How come Grandpa and Aunt Alice didn't join us for Christmas dinner?" There were a few seconds of silence, then Grandma, with no embarrassment at all, said, "Alice and I ain't talkin'!"

Frances cackled in naughty delight. "Hee, hee, hee. They had a fight."

"They did not," Zoan shouted. "Mrs. K--- came here and told Grandpa a lot of stories about you and she told Grandpa an' he said it was a lot of biddy talk 'cause you're a young girl. Then Aunt Alice said, "That red-headed witch is jealous and gossipy and Grandma better not believe her 'cause Daddy needs a wife and we need somebody young around here to liven things up'."

I looked pleadingly at Frank but he was of no help. He was convulsed with silent laughter, flapping his hand helplessly for the children to stop their tattling.

Grandma's eyes flashed. "Ye'll learn that when the

Moseses are mad, they stay mad. Walter's a peace-lovin' soul but that Alice is the youngest in the family of thirteen young-uns and she were spoiled rotten."

"Oh, dear!" I gulped. "I never can stay mad, even when I ought to."

"What do you do when you're mad?" Frances asked, gleefully waiting for a demonstration. She was tiny for seven, too thin, had a wide gap between her new front teeth, her round, blue eyes full of impish expectancy.

"We best all go and have the tree now." Grandma ended the dialogue as matter-of-factly as though none of it had been said.

I was shocked by the lack of joy and enthusiasm as the children opened their presents, and vowed to myself, if I was there for next Christmas, I would make a joyful time of it as I had always known it in my home. The children did not believe in Santa Claus and never had hung their stockings. I assured them I did, and though they snickered, it was plain to see that they were pleased.

Grandma gave each of the little girls a handmade rag doll. I was fascinated by them. They were about twenty inches tall and looked like dolls of a hundred years ago. Their faces were painted on with what appeared to be common household enamel. Their hair was of wool yarn, and each wore a kerchief that matched her flowered, calico jumper. They had white blouses, stiffly starched; long lace-trimmed panties, socks fashioned from stockings, and wool crocheted shoes. Over all this they wore white hamburg aprons, probably cut from the lower half of a Victorian petticoat. Each had a loosely strung necklace of glass beads.

"How unusual and lovely these dolls are! Where did you get the idea or patterns for them, Grandma?" I exclaimed.

"Land sakes. I don't need a pattern," Grandma said. "I've got my own ideas and I've made many a rag baby in my day."

I thought the girls were disappointed that they were not store-bought Shirley Temple dolls, but I was pleased by their polite thanks, though I could understand. The dolls were never actually played with, but were used as decorative pieces for their room.

(Twenty-seven years later, we washed and starched their little clothes and gave them to the Bennington Museum because they looked exactly like many of the little figures in Grandma's famous paintings.)

I had bought skis and poles as my presents. Grandma was exasperated. "You want they should break their legs?"

"I've had skis since I was eight years old, Grandma. I thought it would be fun to teach them. Frank skis, and we can go together," I said. The girls howled with delight.

When the girls had gone out to show the neighbor's kiddies their skis, I went to the kitchen to wash dishes with Grandma. Frank listened to the radio news.

"Why do you think Zoan is so stout when Fran is so painfully thin? Has anyone checked with a doctor?" I asked.

"Jus' natural, I guess. I don't know as Anna ever asked a doctor about it but s'pose she may have. I tried a corset for her last summer but she wouldn't wear it. S'-pose you think she should be on a diet, likely, but you'll never keep her on it. She likes to eat too much."

I wanted to say, "Corset, on that little child?" But instead, "She has such beautiful blonde, curly hair, big blue eyes, a lovely rosy-cheeked clear complexion, and even teeth. She'd be so attractive if only she were twenty pounds lighter."

"Does it bother you?" Grandma wanted to know.

"Yes, I guess it does trouble me. Because it obviously makes her shy and unhappy. Too, I can't believe it is either natural or healthy; her legs are too slender and pretty

34

for a fat person. My sister worked as a dietician at the State House in Boston, as a member of the tubercular clinic for children. I'll ask her to help me."

"You don't say," was Grandma's only comment about that.

Later she said, "Frances is a tease and Zoan falls for it every time. She's Alice's favorite and it makes it hard on Zoan."

"If I marry Frank, I promise I will play no favorites. Frances is cute and comical and smart as a whip. Zoan I find loyal, helpful. She has a keen wit, too. I have a very defensive and protective feeling toward her."

"That's good," said Grandma.

No one could find room for supper, so we nibbled on all Grandma's goodies and played games with the children until Grandma announced, "Early to bed and early to rise," and took them up to bed. She always retired at eight o'clock.

"Do you think Grandma likes me," I asked Frank.

"Your guess is as good as mine. Aunt Mary (Frank never called her 'Grandma') is one fine woman but she's as changeable and temperamental as an artist." (Ah, little did he know.) "I'm right between it with these two old ladies. One pulls me one way, and the other chews my ear off the other. Grandma brought her sister, Ona, here and said she was going to keep house and she'd go home to the farm, but in a few days Ona was gone. I think the children got on her nerves." he sighed. "I'm glad you took that nonsense at the table." We both laughed to think of it.

He looked older than his 34 years: tired, worried, and with deep lines in his face. His shoulders were stooped. He was about six feet tall and dreadfully thin. I longed to say, "I'll come to stay," but held my tongue, keeping my promise to my mother — to think long and carefully.

About midnight we were all in bed. I'd just settled down to go to sleep. The shades were up so that I could see the clear winter sky and sharp, bright stars. I heard a faint click and my doorknob silently, slowly turned. I held my breath and pretended to be asleep, with eyelids open just a slit. Gradually, the door opened about two inches. The streetlight shone through the big windows and caught the rims of Grandma's glasses. She stood, quiet as a mouse, for a matter of half a minute. Softly, gently, the door closed, the knob turned back furtively and caught. I sat up, drew the quilt up to my chin and shivered. I was not frightened, just amazed and puzzled. The brass bed became terribly large and lonely.

As my eyes became accustomed to the semi-darkness, I looked at the high birds-eye maple dresser and noticed that the sepia 8-by-10 photograph of Anna was gone. It had been there the morning I arrived, because I had whispered to it, "Ann, you were pretty. How sad that you should die so young and have to leave Frank, your little daughters, and this new and lovely home. I shall never be jealous of you, just grateful for the girls." Her large sad eyes looked back at me from her high-cheekboned, oval face, her smiling mouth revealing teeth so even and white and perfect, one would almost have thought them false.

"From what I'm told, you're not going to be easy to follow. I'll do my best. Honestly I will."

Letter to my mother. December 28, 1934

"I'm glad you do all like Frank, 'cause I've about decided to marry him. I like a quiet man.

"I still have no idea whether Grandma likes me or not. One minute we're visiting like old relatives, and the next she's sharp with me. Perhaps she doesn't want to like me but does a bit, because I like old people and try to be ultra-respectful.

"Nothing seems to be left out of this house. What closets! Frank's father is not only a dear person, but a master cabinetmaker. I can't wait for you to see the colonial china closet across the corner of the dining room, the linen storage in the upstairs hall and, yes, believe it or not, a cabinet-filled pantry with a nice window. How fortunate to live here with every convenience, if I marry a whole family.

"Frank's Aunt Alice is a professional dressmaker. She has offered to teach me many fine points of sewing. She's younger than Grandma, full of fire and fight, and they don't get on at all. She has white curly hair, cut too short. It stands up in the wind. She was hanging out clothes and Grandma looked out the window. She snorted and said, 'Looks like a dandelion gone to seed.'

"Grandma is embroidering a little oval picture in wool yarns. She's good for a surprise a minute. It's really cute, a Scotch scene. There's a house, trees, and tiny flowers done with silk floss against the wool. She's going to put it in a deep walnut, old, old frame. She says Stuart is a good name and she is glad I'm not a foreigner. Her ancestors were Scotch. Her name was Robertson. When I said how much I liked the picture, she said, 'Good. I'll give it to you for a weddin' present.'

"I said, 'Then you feel you'll be satisfied to have me marry Frank?'

"She said, 'I know you a-goin' to anyways.'

"Well, I said I'd love the picture and would always keep it.

"This morning she took me down to the basement. There's a long row of nice canning cabinets. Every shelf is just full! There must be 250 jars of fruit and vegetables she 'put up' last summer. Plus, there's at least eighty jars of jelly.

"When I showed surprise, she said, 'I s'posed Frank would be gettin' married agin and I'm not about to have anyone find the provision shelves empty.'

"Her son Hugh and his family came to visit yesterday. He is a nice man. He looks much as Ann did, and Frank is very fond of him. I like Dorothy, his wife, and hope she likes me. They have three children. The five kiddies played nicely but were pretty full-of-it. Someone had left a box of Ex-Lax on my windowsill. After they went home, I found the tin box on the floor empty. It scared me and I showed the box to Grandma. She wasn't worried one bit. She laughed and said, 'There's goin' to be one busy backhouse down on the farm.'

"Grandma was most interested to learn that I was born

in Maryland and that you still own the farm near Washington. We had a pleasant morning, she telling me many stories about her life in Staunton, Virginia.

"The children are affectionate with me. That surprises me because I've never seen Grandma even put an arm around them. Maybe she has lost so many she has loved that she's afraid to be too close to them.

"Oh! The questions the children ask me, right in front of Grandma. Today they wanted to know what all of my name was. I hesitated, for Grandma's sake, then said, 'My name is Anne Elizabeth.'

"She gave an awful start and said, 'That beats all.'

"Frances said, 'Swell. My middle name is Elizath (Elizabeth) and Zoan is really Zoeanna, for Daddy's mother and our mother. I bet my mother must-a named us for you.'

"I held my breath, but Grandma roared with laughter and said, 'That's a crazy idee.' She speaks in the strangest, old-fashioned manner and says she never allowed herself to pick up any Southern drawl when she lived there. She calls it 'Darkie lingo.'

"The children want to paint now. Grandma says Frances never knows what her paintings are going to be until she's finished. Grandma showed her how to do mountains and a tree. It was really good. Zoan paints and draws so well that we think she has a decided talent. I want to encourage it."

From my diary. January 1, 1935

Grandma made buckwheat cakes and sausage with maple syrup for breakfast. I never ate such yummy, light buckwheat cakes. Grandma insists they're not as good without Virginia buckwheat honey. She gave me the recipe.

Grandma Moses's Buckwheat Pancakes
    2 cups of buckwheat flour
    3/4 cup all-purpose flour
    1 teaspoon salt
    1 teaspoon soda dissolved in a little warm water
    Make a batter and let it stand overnight where it's cold but not freezing (in other words, not in a farm buttery).
    In the morning, add enough buttermilk to pour well off a spoon. Have griddle hot and always use a piece of salt pork to grease the griddle.

41

Grandma says I may have an old black leather notebook of hers, with recipes she collected from kinfolks and neighbors, years ago. In the front of the cookbook, someone with a marvelous handwriting had written their Sunday school lessons. I asked Grandma whose writing it was and she said, "Guess it musta been Zoe's. She's the only one who was very religious in the family. Thomas and I never held to much church goin' Walter don't neither, but Zoe did right as she see it and took her boys regular. Anna sent the girls to the Episcopal Sunday School, so I do. Are you church goin'?

"Yes. I belong to a nonsectarian church. I sing in the choir."

"Well, now, that's a new outfit to me. Where do you get your highfalutin talk?"

"What did I say that's highfalutin?"

"I mind as you say, 'Larf' instead of 'Laf.' "

"Everyone speaks with a broad 'A' around Boston. I'll probably get over it when I live in Vermont a while."

"I don't know as you should," she chuckled. "It does sound sorta high-toned."

January 2, 1935. From my diary

At last, Grandma let me help. I washed the dishes and ironed the children's dresses. She was sewing buttonholes in pajamas for Hugh's kids. She kept sighing and looking at me and finally said,

"There's a few things I s'pose I ought to tell you about the men in the Moses outfit. My brother, Fred, says he's found out you come by a good family, no finer woman than ya mother and no lickers allowed. First off, the Moses don't want their woman to handle money. Oh, they're generous enough, Thomas and Walter never did refuse their woman anything reasonable. As I've said, they're awful good providers. Walter don't drink only a little cider, now and agin, but his boys both drink some. They hold it good. They like their game of cards, too, but Anna never had complaint."

"What I want to know, can I trust Frank to be sober, honest, and truthful?"

"He's honest enough," she said flatly.

"Do you think I can make a success of marriage and being a mother here? If I cannot take on this job when times are so hard, do I deserve to do so later, after going to college? Don't they all need me most now?"

43

"You'll seem like a mighty energetic girl ta me. I guess you'll do."

(That is all Grandma had to say about me in her books after she became famous: "Frank married an energetic girl for his second wife.")

January 3, 1935. From my diary

I have a touch of the flu. Grandma has me in bed and trots up and down stairs, bringing me homemade tomato juice and hot catnip tea. She just insisted on changing the bed.

"I don't want you should smell like a nest of puppies," she said when I didn't want to make her extra work. What comical old sayings she uses. Yesterday she was telling me about a neighbor they had in Eagle Bridge. She said, "He's as close as the next second, wouldn't pay a nickel to see an earthquake."

I said, "I'm afraid you'll catch this flu bug. Maybe you shouldn't come in here near me."

"Oh. Pshaw," she exclaimed. "Only you young folks git sick. I got no time for that nonsense." She perched on the edge of the window seat and began to visit.

"I s'pose you and Frank will want young-uns of yer own; then how'll you feel about the girls?"

"Why, Grandma, they'll all be sisters and brothers. That should make us closer. I'll certainly try never to give our girls reasons for jealousy. Stepmothers are for old fairy tales. We'll all love tiny babies."

A faraway look came into her eyes, a look of bitterness, and an expression of past sorrow mixed with stoic acceptance.

"I lost five babies, you know. I got so's I felt they was only a loan, if they lived at all. When Totzie — that's Hugh — came along we didn't even give him a name till he was most eight months old. Some folks blamed Thomas 'cause the babies come so clos't together, but I always said, 'It takes two to turkey-trot.' Thomas was the best man ever lived," She slid down and went to the top of the stairs and called down to the children, "You stop that janglin' before one of you gits hurt." She popped back into the room and hitched herself back upon the window seat. "Loyd and Forrest was the same space in age as these two, and they was at it half the time. Forrest was younger but he always wanted to be boss; and Onee (Winona), she couldn't stand neither of 'um."

I didn't interrupt at any point of her story, fearful that I might distract her or perhaps close the door of her compassionate moments with me.

"Once'st there was an awful outbreak of childbed fever. 'Bout every other woman who birthed died of it. A terrible death it was, too. I was light (I had never heard that expression but am told by older women that it was frequently used in Grandma's day for "pregnant") for one of those that was stillborn an' I was plenty nerved-up, as were Thomas. Wan't a soul that knew what brought it on, in them days. I believe it was the worst lay-in I ever had. It stormed somethin' fearful that night. I'll never forgit it. We had a washbench out by the back door on the stoop and my washtub hung to one side of the buildin'. It went bang, bang, bang, all night long. Along toward daybreak Thomas says, 'Is there anything I can do for you, Mary?' He couldn't see I was real fussed and he had to be about the chores a-spell. I said, 'Yes, there is! Will you go take that blame washtub down so's I kin git some peace in my labor?' He was real surprised but he rushed out and tended to it an' I didn't have to hear that thumpin' any more."

"All's I have to help me that time was a fat old darkie woman, we called Aunt Peachie. She was real clean and a good soul. She'd acted right scared an' her a-pern over her head, 'cause she said she'd been sure that tub knockin' on the wall was the spirits comin' to git me. Those dark-ies were always afeard of hants."

"After Thomas took the little body away to be buried, I was real poorly. I asked Aunt Peachie if she thought maybe I'd be dyin' of the fever."

"She said, 'You ought to git up and let all that stink stuff come on out of you. Indians gits right up and walks and they don't never gits the child-bed fevers.' I was so weak. I couldn't of made a hummin' bird a pair of garters, but I got up and she walked me about the bed. Every day, after that, I got up and walked some and my strength come back real fast. I never told Thomas what I was up to, it would have scared him to death, most. T'wasn't ladylike or safe to git out of child-bed before two weeks. (Grandma lived to see that Aunt Peachie's theory was correct.)

From my diary. January 6, 1935

Pepperell, Massachusetts

I came home today. It was hard to see Frank go back to Vermont alone. We've decided to be married on his birthday, April 6. (We actually were married on Febru-ary 8, 1935, because Grandma just decided she was going home, and that was that.) Before I left, I told Grandma and she seemed to approve.

She said, "What are ya waitin' fer?"

I said, "Frank and I think it would be nice and only right that you stay here through the rest of this bitter cold weather because there is only stove heat on the farm."

"Hummmm!" she answered.

The little girls cried and wanted to know why it took so long to get married.

Grandma said, "You needn't think to inconvenience me, because the sooner the better, so far as I'm concerned. I got things to do. East-West, own home's best."

I wonder what on earth she's so anxious to do. I never saw anyone in their seventies as full of ambition. I surely do admire her. She's so busy all the time, she doesn't know she's old, and wouldn't be bored if she were on a desert island. She'd probably make a picture with sand pebbles. (Now there's a prophesy for you.)

Thirty-eight years later

How little did anyone dream of all Grandma was to do! She walked with kings and visited presidents, knew how to relish fame and fortune, and lived to be 101.

"Only young folks gits sick."

We are always amused to hear her described as a frail little old lady. Bent and tiny though she was, she was fire, steel, and strength, articulate for one so limited in education, brave enough to bear, with patience and submission, the loss of Anna, Ona, and Hugh.

When Hugh died of a heart attack without a second's warning, Frank spoke to comfort her.

She said, "You just have to learn, Frank, that these things happen. You'll have to excuse me, lots of folks are comin' and I've got a turkey in to roast."

Grandma found her comfort and salvation in the joy of work. There was no job she attacked — and I use that word intentionally — that she didn't find worth doing well. Her determination was unequalled, and she was never defeated on any ground until she was placed in a nursing home.

Louis Bromfield expressed it best when he said, "She is a wise, shrewd and happy old lady, who loves life and color."

The Landscape of Eagle Bridge

A series of photographs that evoke the fields, farms, and woodland scenes that Grandma Moses painted.

photographs by Tyler Resch

Chronology

Anna Mary Robertson "Grandma" Moses and Beth Moses Hickok (née Anne Elizabeth Stuart)

1860, Sept. 7   Anna Mary Robertson (called "Mary" by her family) is born on a farm in Greenwich, N.Y.

1872 — 1887   Mary Robertson leaves home to earn a living as a hired girl on a neighboring farm, continues working on other farms.

1887, Nov. 9   Mary marries Thomas Salmon Moses, a farmer who was born in Hoosick, N.Y. They move to Staunton, Va., in the Shenandoah Valley.

1887 — 1905   Thomas and Mary Moses rent a series of farms in Virginia and buy two, in 1896 and 1903. During this time they have ten children, of whom five survive infancy: Winona (called Ona), Loyd, Forrest, Anna, and Hugh.

1905   After their farmhouse in Staunton burns, the Moses family returns to their home territory; they buy a dairy farm in Eagle Bridge, a village in the town of Hoosick, N.Y., not far from the Vermont border.

1911, Sept. 25   Anne Elizabeth Stuart (the author of this book) is born in Hyattsville, Md.; when she is about five years old, her family moves to Pepperell, Mass., northwest of Boston.

1927, Jan. 15   Thomas Salmon Moses dies.

1927 — 1929   Mary (now "Grandma") Moses begins caring for her ailing daughter, Anna (Mrs. Frank Moses) on Elm Street in Bennington, Vt. Anna improves for a time, then her condition (tuberculosis) worsens so that by 1929 Grandma has moved in to keep house for her son-in-law and to care for granddaughters Zoan and Frances. Grandma works on yarn or worsted paintings.

1932, autumn   Beth Stuart leaves home in Pepperell to take a job as a rural telephone operator in Dorset, Vt.

1933, Feb. 5   Anna Moses dies and is buried in the plot of her father-in-law, Walter Moses, in Park Lawn Cemetery, Bennington.

1934, March 27   Beth meets the widower Frank Moses.

1934, Dec. 25   Beth arrives to spend Christmas holidays in Bennington with Frank and his daughters and experiences the ten days with Grandma Moses that form the text of this book.

1935, Jan. 6   Beth returns home to Pepperell, having decided to marry Frank.

1935, Feb. 8   Beth and Frank Moses marry. Grandma Moses is free to return to the farm in Eagle Bridge. Artistic all her life, she begins to paint in earnest in different media — with yarn, house paint on pine boards, etc., and exhibits her work along with her preserves at county fairs.

1936 and 1938   Frank and Beth Moses's children Gail and Hank are born.

1938, Eastertime   Grandma Moses's primitive paintings are "discovered" by art collector Louis J. Caldor of New York City in the window of W. D. Thomas's drugstore in Hoosick Falls, N.Y.

1939, autumn   Three of her paintings are shown at the Museum of Modern Art's exhibit, "Contemporary Unknown American Painters."

1940   Grandma Moses has a solo show, titled "What a Farm Wife Painted," at Otto Kallir's Galerie St. Etienne on West 57th Street in New York. She continues to gain fame over the next two decades and her talent develops.

1960, Sept. 7   Grandma Moses's 100th birthday is marked as a virtual day of national celebration.

1961, Dec. 13   Grandma Moses dies at the age of 101 years, 3 months, 6 days, at the Hoosick Falls Health Center, and is buried in Maple Grove Cemetery, Hoosick Falls, N.Y. Inscription on her headstone reads, "Her primitive paintings captured the spirit and preserved the scene of a vanishing countyside."

1962, winter   Beth Moses writes the final paper for her three-year correspondence course (Famous Writers School), and titles it "Ten Days With Grandma Moses."

1971, March 31   Frank Moses dies, is buried next to his first wife, Anna, in Park Lawn Cemetery.

"*Remembering Grandma Moses*" *is an active enterprise in Hoosick Falls, New York, near her own hamlet of Eagle Bridge. On the side of a windowless three-story brick building in downtown Hoosick Falls there appears a gigantic version of her painting titled Wagon Repair Shop. This photo was taken in August 1993 when artist Roger Weeden had been engaged to refurbish the painting's colors which had faded in several years of sunlight. Not far away, at the top of a hill in the Maple Grove Cemetery just east of Hoosick Falls, is found Grandma Moses's grave. Here she is remembered by the inscription, "Her primitive paintings captured the spirit and preserved the scene of a vanishing countryside."*